LIVING A 5-STAR LIFE BY DESIGN

Eight Biblical and Business Principles
For Enjoying A Lifestyle of Quality

Sharon L. Jordan

Xulon
PRESS

This book is dedicated to:

My Heavenly Father

My First Fruit

Contents

✳ ✳ ✳ ✳ ✳

Chapter 1

What Is A 5-Star Life?

*"Beloved, I pray that you may prosper in all things
and be in health, just as your soul prospers."*
3 John 2 (NKJV)

*"Invest in the human soul.
Who knows, it might be a diamond in the rough."*
Mary McLeod Bethune

Earning a 5-Star rating is the pursuit of any restaurant or hotel that desires to have a reputation for quality. A 5-Star rating is a category where an establishment has been considered to be top-notch, first rated, the A+, a class above all others. A 5-Star rating symbolizes that an establishment's quality has been noticed by customers and customers do not mind paying extra money for the services provided.

Quality, as defined by the American Heritage is "a degree or grade of excellence." Quality, from a customer's perceptive, is expected. Quality, however, from the supplier's perspective, doesn't occur by happenstance or by the luck of the draw. Quality is a step-by-step, rigorous approach to building superiority into a product or service. Quality separates the good from the best.

After World War II, the United States lost focus on quality and allowed Japan to welcome and embrace two American citizens, W. Edward Deming and Joseph M. Juran, to rebuild and reposition Japan as a nation of quality.

Deming preached a fourteen-point quality system that could propel any company or nation to a place of quality prominence. Deming's focus was on statistical quality control which was in conflict with America's current system of inspection. Deming's fourteen-point quality structure, described by William W. Scherkenbach, is:

- Create constancy of purpose toward improvement of product and service.
- Adopt the new philosophy. We are in a new economic age.

- Cease dependence on mass inspection to achieve quality.
- Constantly and forever improve the system.
- Remove barriers.
- Drive out fear.
- Break down barriers between departments.
- Eliminate numerical goals.
- Eliminate work standards (quotas).
- Institute modern methods of supervision.
- Institute modern methods of training.
- Institute a program of education and retraining.
- End the practice of awarding business on price tag.
- Put everybody in the company to work to accomplish the transformation.

Joseph Juran's contribution to quality was different from Deming. Juran's concept focused on managing quality. Juran named human or cultural resistance as the root cause of quality issues in America. Juran's trilogy—planning, control and improvement—is an acceptable approach for quality management.

Japan became a nation known for quality because they embraced the philosophies of Deming and Juran.

Shocked from Japan's quality and subsequent impact on American business, the United States began to take a look at repositioning itself in regards to Quality. The result was a term called "total quality management (TQM)." TQM focused on how an entire organization could improve its processes to yield a quality product.

In 1989, the International Organization for Standardization (ISO) developed a criterion for quality management to which a customer could expect a quality product. ISO is a Greek word meaning "equal." The implication of ISO is that anyone who embraces and practices these standards could expect excellent execution in all functionality of products and services.

As I became knowledgeable and involved in the tools of quality, I found myself using these same tools in my personal life. I discovered that my life took on a whole different concept and level of excellence that I never experienced.

I, by nature, am a lazy, carefree person. I concurred with Jerry Brown that "Life Just Is." Lay back and let things happen. As I implemented the quality tools that will be shared with you in this book, I discovered that I had some say in the shaping of my life.

While learning the quality tools needed to perform my secular work, I was constantly nudged by the Holy Spirit of the biblical principles that I had learned as a child. Having the biblical foundation of quality, I discovered that my Heavenly Father, from the foundations of the earth, wanted and planned so much more for my life. It was through working in the quality field that moved my personal existence toward designing my *5-Star Life.*

Quality management's agenda is to plan, execute, and manage processes that will add value to the customer and for a business. This book's agenda is to share with you quality management principles, both biblical and business, that will increase value in your personal life and to those you come in contact with.

Think about it. Your life is a business that, every day, every hour and every second is engaged in transactions. The American Heritage Dictionary defines transaction as *"to do, carry on, or conduct."* Time is a precious commodity. We can capitalize it or squander it. Ephesians chapter 5 verse sixteen puts out the clarion cry:

Making the very most of the time [buying up each opportunity], because the days are evil. (AMP)

As you read this book, you are engaged in a transaction of time. The exchange, hopefully, is to understand how to move towards living a *5-Star Life by Design.* As we begin to understand the value of time, we are made aware of the cost of our choices and options.

To embark on this *5-Star Life by Design* will require work. I am a believer in miracles. However, I understand the discipline of healing. Miracles are supernatural events that God works that go against the law of nature. The feeding of 5000 men as recorded in Mark chapter six verses forty one through forty four illustrates a miracle:

And when he had taken the five loaves and the two fishes, he looked up to heaven, and blessed, and brake the loaves, and gave *them* to his disciples to set before them; and the two fishes divided he among them all. And they did all eat, and were filled. And they took up twelve baskets full of the fragments, and of the fishes. And they that did eat of the loaves were about five thousand men.

Healing, on the other hand, is a natural progression of events that restores things to its rightful position. Healing involves a person to participate in natural steps that result in the finish objective. Second Thessalonians chapter three verses ten through twelve expresses a natural occurrence of things:

> **Don't you remember the rule we had when we lived with you? "If you don't work, you don't eat." And now we're getting reports that a bunch of lazy good-for-nothings are taking advantage of you. This must not be tolerated. We command them to get to work immediately—no excuses, no arguments—and earn their own keep. (MSG)**

A *5-Star Life by Design* is a healing process. It will take work and effort on our part to realize the end results. This book will help you do just that by expounding on eight biblical and biblical quality principles.

Visioning is the concept of dreaming your wildest dreams. Visioning invites us to go back to our childhood era and bring back to our remembrance the desires of what we expected out of life. Visioning will mandate that we see what the end result of our *5-Star Life* resembles.

Planning is where we focus on strategies that will help us realize the vision of our *5-Star Life*. Planning requires that we put forth purposeful effort, through goals and measurements, to accomplish the tasks that move us toward the *5-Star Life* that we visualize.

Documenting Procedures require that we devise the blueprint of our *5-Star Life*. This will be imposing but important. The outcome will serve as a map for moving us to the quality lifestyle we mandate.

Process Management is the potency of standardization. Process management makes us perceptive of the workings of a process and presses us to proceed in a particular manner. Developing *5-Star* habits is a more familiar term.

Systems Management challenges us to move from silo thinking to systems thinking. Silo thinking is where things work independently. The world has conditioned us to believe that we are independent. Not so! Everything is linked and interdependent. We will be challenged to discover the linkages that will lead to a *5-Star Life by Design.*

Internal Audits analyze if we are doing what we are saying (or documenting). The objective of auditing is to confirm compliance of our actions that move us toward our *5-Star Life.* Undergoing an audit requires an explicit examination of our actions to determine and decide if we are, in fact, making progress toward our *5-Star Life by Design.*

Corrective Actions presents opportunities to improve the activities that we established to realize our *5-Star Life by Design.* Correcting actions provides us the leverage to hone or sharpen our focus on end-results that provides a great payoff.

Finally, Cost of Quality challenges us to consider if we want to invest in a *5-Star Life by Design.* Like any business venture, there is a benefit and loss evaluation that takes place to help with the decision to undergo an adventure. This chapter will present the thoughts of the writer of what we can and cannot expect from the biblical and business tools presented.

Each chapter ends with a *Quest for Quality* section. The Quest for Quality is activating questions that only you can answer. There is no right or wrong answer. The queries are meant to inspire, motivate and move you toward the *5-Star Life* you've always dreamt about. The activities are a living work. Perfection is not required. However, serious thought should be given to build the foundation of your *5-Star Life.*

How about it? Let's get to work on our *5-Star Life by Design.*

Chapter 2

The Principle of Visioning: Seeing A 5-Star Life

❧❧❧

"...I came that they may have and enjoy life, and have it in abundance (to the full, till it overflows)."
John 10:10b (AMP)

"The best way to predict the future is to create it."
Peter Drucker

L iving a **5-Star Life by Design** begins with vision. Steven R. Covey, in his bestseller *The 7 Habits of Highly Effective People*, encapsulates the ministry of visualization in his second habit: *Begin with the end in mind.* Where do you want your life to go? What effect do you want your life to produce? Do you want a life of truth or hypocrisy? Do you desire a life of purpose or pomp? What do you want others to say about you once you are dead and gone?

Proverbs chapter twenty nine verse eighteen says **"Where there is no vision, the people perish."** Let us rephrase this verse to make it personal: Where there is no vision, I perish." The word *perish* in the American Heritage dictionary means to "t*o die or be destroyed, especially in a violent or untimely manner; to pass from existence; disappear gradually."* What a sad state of affairs to have the capacity to live a wonderful and fulfilling life all to see it waste away because vision was not cast for our lives. We can change that and so we shall. We start by visioning our destiny.

Vision is vital. First, vision is needed to control our destiny. We can have power over our destiny or we can allow outside forces to have power over us. Vision gives us a sense of direction to where we are headed. Vision prevents us from an itinerant life of wondering and aimlessness.

Secondly, vision is vital to allow us to picture our future. The mind is a powerful tool that God gave us. It is in the imagination of the mind where thoughts of good and evil are conjured up. The images that play in our imagination tremendously impact the realties that we create. Proverbs chapter 23 verse 7 says **"For as he thinketh in his heart, so is he."**

Thirdly, vision is vital because vision isn't based on facts or logic. Vision is desire driven where we can create and reinvent the course of our lives. Vision extends us the invitation to picture our wildest dreams! When the dark and dismal days of living pounce upon us, vision reminds us that life is worth living. Our vision does not have to inspire anybody. However, it must inspire us.

My vision was inspired while studying a passage of scripture found in Exodus chapter one verse nineteen. This passage of scripture tells the story of how the Israelites were increasing so abundantly that the Pharaoh of Egypt began to seek ways to destroy them. The Pharaoh was unaware that a Hebrew slave, Joseph, was used by Jehovah God to save the land of Egypt from the effects of a severe famine. This Joseph was made second in command to lead Egypt through the dearth.

Fearing this nation of people, The Pharaoh had commanded the Egyptian midwives to kill every male child born to the Israeli women. Since the midwives feared God, they did not obey Pharaoh's command. When the Pharaoh asked why his command was not being obeyed, the midwives responded that the Hebrew women were not like the Egyptian women. The midwives used an adjective that caught my attention: *lively.*

The word *"lively"* as defined in Strong's Greek & Hebrew Dictionary, comes from a primitive root *Chayah* (pronounced ha-yaa*).* It means *"to live, to revive, to give (promise) life, nourish up, preserve (alive), quicken, recover, repair, restore (to life), revive, to be whole."* I felt like neither of these adjectives when I read this definition. Yet, the word resonated in my spirit. My vision was birthed. I began to declare "I am a *Chayah* Woman!"

What resonates in you that brings out life in you? Begin to be conscious of the stirrings in your heart. Vision starts with a "gut feeling" that can only be recognized by you.

Where Are You Going?

Space, the final frontier. ... Its five-year mission: To explore strange new worlds. To seek out new life and new civilizations. To boldly go where no man has gone before.

This is the mission statement of the starship *Enterprise.* This mission statement was announced at the beginning of every television show. And the television show delivered on its promise. Today, thousands of people are loyal fans of Star Trek.

A famous Jewish carpenter's mission statement is found in Saint Luke chapter four verses nineteen and twenty:

The Spirit of the Lord is upon me, because he hath anointed me to preach the gospel to the poor; he hath sent me to heal the brokenhearted, to preach deliverance to the captives, and recovering of sight to the blind, to set at liberty them that are bruised, To preach the acceptable year of the Lord.

Throughout Jesus' life, his actions were steered by his powerful mission. He changed the course of the universe because he stayed the course that governed his life.

A mission statement charts your course. It is a convincing and credible future for your life. A mission statement lays the foundation for visioning your life, defining your purpose, establishing values that dictate your behavior, setting goals to pursue, and determining accurate measurements to keep you on track. Galatians chapter six verses four and five in the Message Bible states:

Make a careful exploration of who you are and the work you have been given, and then sink yourself into that. Don't be impressed with yourself. Don't compare yourself with others. Each of you must take responsibility for doing the creative best you can with your own life.

In *Full Steam Ahead* the book opens up at the funeral of one of the main characters, Jim Carpenter. His eulogy, read by his daughter, was written by Jim years ago. The eulogy was, in fact, Jim's personal mission statement. Jim's mission statement was his "vision" of how he wanted people to remember him by. Therefore, he was driven and guided by his personal mission statement.

A simple definition of a mission statement is what one feels called to do. It should encapsulate the essence of where you are going. An effective mission statement must resonate within you. It must arouse originality, obedience, and obstinacy.

A mission statement is written down so that you can refer back to it. What you commit to writing is easier to remember and act upon. God instructed his prophet to write vision down as a way of reminding people of things to come because vision dies if it is left neglected.

And then God answered: "Write this. Write what you see. Write it out in big block letters so that it can be read on the run. This vision-message is a witness pointing to what's coming. It aches for the coming—it can hardly wait! And it doesn't lie. If it seems slow in coming, wait. It's on its way. It will come right on time. Habakkuk 2:2-3 (MSG)

What's Driving Your Destiny

The American Heritage dictionary defines purpose as "the object toward which one strives or for which something exists." Rick Warren's best seller *The Purpose Driven Life* motivated millions to look at life from fifty thousand feet instead of the five feet in which many of us operate. Looking at life from fifty thousand feet means to see how we fit together as a system and not from individual silos.

Mark Sanborn's *The Fred Factor* is an inspiring book on how a postal worker named Fred made it his business to give extraordinary customer service to the customers he served. Fred, the postal worker, had a personal mission that fueled him to live an extraordinary life. Fred's purpose was not to just deliver mail. Fred saw his life as a communication link between people.

This is what I believe purpose is. Purpose is not in the actions we do or the jobs we perform. Purpose is discovering and defining what business we really are in.

How exactly do we find out what we are to be and do? Good question! As I stated earlier, our "gut feeling" is a quarry for knowing purpose. As we begin to seek the purpose for our lives, purpose will impress itself on us.

Many of our lives are filled with many activities. We are busy doing and not being. Every day, I would compile my list of "things to do." It was filled with activities. One day as I was compiling my list, my thoughts led me into conversation as to why I never wrote down my list of "things to be." This was a revelation moment for me.

I began a period of fasting and praying to seek God for the purpose in which I took up space on planet Earth. Being a Quality Analyst by trade, I was incessant in finding out my purpose. I was plagued with "Analysis Paralysis." This is a term used when one gets so wrapped up in analyzing things that it prevents one from ever producing anything worth value.

One evening while leaving work, I looked up at the sky and asked God "what is my purpose?" The words came back sternly: "Just start living!" I started laughing as revelation came: *"If you start something, I (God) will show you something."*

Sounds like faith, doesn't it. Faith does not require us to see. Faith requires us to act when we don't see.

I began to study my life. What activities did I participate in that "lit my fire," that I was passionate about, that I made time for, that I invested my money in? The greatest life we can live is a life that lights us up so that we can give light to others. Matthew chapter five verse seventeen instructs us to **"let our light so shine before men that they see.."** Our *5-Star Life by Design* should be lights that excites!

- ❧ I discovered that I love to teach people what I know. An indescribable feeling envelopes me when someone is empowered because of something I said or showed them.
- ❧ I discovered that I like to do things differently. I am bored easily. I like to bring my own twist to projects and programs.
- ❧ I discovered that I like to be by myself. I like to have the house to myself so that I can read and think.
- ❧ I enjoy socializing with people. I am amazed at what I learn from people who are not like me.

As I answered these questions, my purpose came forth:

I am purposed to create, nurture and teach others through the careful balance of self.

How You Do What You Do

The third leg of the mission statement is values. The American Heritage dictionary defines value as *a principle, standard, or quality considered worthwhile or desirable.* Values determine how we will operate our lives. Values determine the behaviors that we will utilize to operate our daily affairs. The manner by which we choose to live will determine the reputation and legacy we leave behind. Deliberate consideration must be given to determine the core values that will assist us in our *5-Star Life by Design.*

Jesus' first public discourse dealt with values. Within His teachings on the Sermon of the Mount, as told in Matthew chapters five through chapter seven, Jesus showcases some core values and the reward of implementing them. This lesson teaches us that whatever values we choose to embrace, a consequence will follow.

Values guide us as we pursue our purpose. I have this quote by Henry Ward Beecher on my office desk:

> *Hold yourself responsible for a higher standard than anybody else expects of you. Never excuse yourself. Never pity yourself. Be a hard master to yourself— and be lenient to everybody else.*

Beecher's quote is a daily reminder that my *5-Star Life by Design* is my responsibility. I cannot blame anyone for the lack of discipline or values that keep me from my personal best.

Living a *5-Star Life by Design* is value-driven. Values supply the power, direction and command that propels our purpose. Values work in a similar manner as a Global Positioning System (GPS). My husband purchased an automobile for me. The automobile was built with a GPS. It took me five months before I tried it out. As I was planning a trip to a conference in another city, I decided to see how the GPS worked. All I needed to do was enter the address of my destination. The GPS voice spoke to tell me that the system was calculating my position and determining the direction in which I was to travel. The voice spoke again and said "at the stop sign, make a right turn." I followed the command. The voice spoke again "at the stop sign, make a right turn." I obeyed. The GPS eventually led me to the city where the conference was being held. When I arrived got to the city, I missed a turn. The voice told me that the system was rerouting me to where I needed to be. Values, like the GPS, determine the route we will take in living a *5-Star Life by Design.*

We must establish clear values. These values will be our guiding principles that determine our actions, decision, and behaviors. Values will determine the difference between the boring and the brilliant, the mundane and the magnificent, the ordinary and the extraordinary, and the blessed and not so blessed.

Ben Franklin's life is one worth modeling when it comes to establishing and practicing personal values. Mr. Franklin at the age of twenty established thirteen personal values that he modeled his life's actions after. It is interesting to note that Ben Franklin was one of the founding fathers who carved out the Constitution of the United States. The Constitution of the United States is the guiding principles for the citizens of the United States. Mr. Franklin's private deliberations of his personal values paved the way for him to publicly deliberate values for this new nation called the United States of America.

What values or principles do you hold in esteem? Is trustworthiness an honorable trait to you? Is integrity and honesty? What about morality or ethics? Understanding and wisdom? Self-respect? What do you want to be known for? Isaiah chapter thirty two verse eight in the Message Bible says **"But those who are noble make noble plans, and stand for what is noble."**

Establishing personal values is not an easy task. It takes quality time to reflect and discover our true beliefs and what is really important to us. Things that we think are important give way to the wind when we weigh it against personal risk.

Here is the acid test of a guiding principle: *What would you risk your life for?*

When I began my **5-Star Life by Design**, I originally started with eight guiding principles. It took me twelve hours to develop. I was surprised at what I discovered about myself. So that you can have an example of writing your guiding principles, I expose mine to you:

1. I share this earthly trek with Richard L. Jordan. I am committed to solve the mystery of becoming one with him. I communicate my needs and desires to him in such a way that brings harmony to my spirit, to our relationship and to our home.

2. I am a loving and nurturing mother to Larry, James, Devin and Reva. Since these four are my most valued gifts from God, I commit therefore to motherhood in such a way that instructs and raise them in the reverential fear of the Lord. I help bring out their natural abilities in order for them to be contributing adults in the world.

3. I make sound decisions. I inquire of the Lord of the Universe for direction and take immediate action for God's Word tells me that "He will direct my path."

4. I am organized. I plan each activity with rigor and clarity. I follow through and meet all deadlines. I

33

effectively eliminate wasted activities that deter me from reaching my goals.

5. I am physically fit. I eat that which is nutritious and beneficial to my body. I exercise regularly, knowing that my body is the temple of the Holy Spirit.

6. I am financially sound. I am knowledgeable about my household financial picture. I pay my tithes and offerings. Therefore, money cometh to me!

7. I am ever increasing in wisdom and knowledge. I put into practice the disciplines needed to maximize my personal best.

8. I speak the truth in love.

No way have I mastered these values. However, I declare and decree these values daily in my morning prayers. As I go about my day, I am consciously aware of these values. My behavior and actions align to what I think and speak.

Your values will not be mine. You may have more. You may have less. The goal is not to be a copycat. You are a unique individual, created for a unique purpose. Discover that uniqueness and you will be on your way to living your *5-Star Life by Design*!

Quest for Quality

Visioning is vital to living a 5-Star Life.

Close your eyes. See yourself living a *5-Star Life.*
Allow yourself to feel the emotions associated with
living your dream. Be thankful for the blessing of
living your *5-Star Life.*

A Mission Statement is a brief statement that provides direction and purpose.

Describe on paper what you see. What activities are
you performing that are associated with your *5-Star
Life*? At your death, what do you want people to
remember about you?

Values determine how you operate your *5-Star Life.* They
are deep-seated beliefs that guide our decisions and behaviors. Values are learned and are personally integrated into
your life.

Determine what you want your value system to be.
What values do you need to discard?
What values do you need to work on?

Chapter 3

The Principle of Planning: Strategies for a 5-Star Life

෴

"…Let us rise up and build.
So they strengthened their hands for this good
work." Nehemiah 2:18c

"Do-so is more important than say-so"
Peter Seeger

L ife is a journey. You can travel it in one or two ways: prepared or unprepared. I started the unprepared way.

For example, I once told my husband that I wanted to go to New York. He, being the Prepared Traveler, told me to plan the trip. I looked at him and responded that I didn't need to prepare. "All we need to do is get on I-77N to I-76E and follow the sign to New York (I think it is I-80)." He asked me what plans were made for the hotel accommodations. I told him we would find a hotel when we got there. Needless to say, the Prepared Traveler didn't buy into my strategy.

Looking back, my idea was foolish. But at the time, I was dead serious. The same approach I reasoned for the trip to New York is the same way many of us approach life: Unplanned, unprepared, unproductive, and unpromising.

The act of planning creates a format or a proposal to accomplish or attain something. I would have had better buy-in from the Prepared Traveler to visit New York if I had approached him with a plan of action that agreed with him. The plan would include information such as what part of New York to visit, departure date, arrival date, travel arrangements, costs, and attractions to take in.

Preparing consists of making the details beforehand. If we were driving, a call to AAA for driving directions and maps of the city would be necessary. If time and cost were factors, air travel arrangements would need to be made.

Hotel reservations need to be arranged. Ticketed events must be purchased. Did I figure out a budget?

If the planning and preparing activities are careful, concise and clear, the itinerary will be more productive and practical to my Prepared Traveler and going to New York will be more promising!

A *5-Star Life by Design* is a life of planning, preparing, and producing. Nothing less. Look at any company around you. The companies that are growing are the companies that are constantly planning, preparing and producing. The product is a promise for potential profit.

The major obstacle for not experiencing a *5-Star Life by Design* is our failure to set goals. I, like many others, was too carefree with my life. Being a Christian, I thought everything would magically appear as long as I was doing the "Christian" things of praying, reading my scripture, attending church services and paying my tithes. These activities are good and very needful, but I did not have revelation of the need for goals.

Each January 1, I would make New Year's resolutions. I found time to be alone to write down what I wanted to accomplish for the New Year. My list went something like this:

- Lose weight
- Save money
- Buy a brown suit (no kidding)
- Keep the house clean
- Be nice to my husband and children
- Entertain at home

I tucked the list away. By February, I had forgotten about the list. What I was missing was goal setting.

A goal, according to the American Heritage dictionary, is *"the purpose toward which an endeavor is directed."* With goals come planning. The American Heritage dictionary defines planning as *"to formulate a scheme or program for the accomplishment, enactment, or attainment of."* Without goal planning, we have no direction.

Michael Jordan would not be known as a great basketball player had it not been for his goal to be one. Patty LaBelle would not be known as an awesome performer had it not been for her ambition to be one. Donald Trump would not be known as a successful businessman had it not been his intent to be one. Sharon Jordan would not be known as a prolific writer had it not been her aim to be one! Get my point?.

One of my sons plays football. Before his games I would observe his "pregame" activities. Of course, he would eat. But his favorite activity was to watch prior games of his team. He would sit in front of the television reviewing games they won and lost. I asked him why he did this. He commented that he wanted to strengthen the good plays he made and reduce the not-so-good plays. He would tell me that his goal was to be a better receiver than the prior games. He stated that he has to see himself catching the balls and making the touchdowns way before he ever got on the field. As of this writing, he holds many records at his high school in the wide receiver category.

Revelation time: Just as my son set his goals before the game, we, too, should prepare and set goals for our lives.

Following God's Lead

Our Creator God has set the pattern for us to follow. God has plans:

> **What I have said, that will I bring about; what I have planned, that will I do.** Isaiah 46.11c (NIV)

> **Before I shaped you in the womb, I knew all about you. Before you saw the light of day, I had holy plans for you: A prophet to the nations— that's what I had in mind for you.** Jeremiah 1.5 (MSG)

> **For I know the thoughts *and* plans that I have for you, says the Lord, thoughts *and* plans for welfare *and* peace and not for evil, to give you hope in your final outcome.** Jeremiah 29:11 (AMP)

God wants to be involved in our goals and help us accomplish our goals:

> **Roll your works upon the Lord [commit and trust them wholly to Him; He will cause your thoughts to become agreeable to His will, and] so shall your plans be established *and* succeed.** Proverbs 16:3 (AMP)

> **May He grant you according to your heart's desire and fulfill all your plans.** Psalms 20:4 (AMP).

Many of us do not set goals. We aimlessly go through life waiting on things to happen to us. We unconsciously live out the adage "people don't plan to fail, they fail to plan." We are bad managers when it comes to controlling our time and life. Ephesians chapter five verse sixteen instructs us to "redeem the time." The word redeem is used in reference to money or value. Time is money. Time is valuable. We place a low value on our time when we fail to plan our lives.

We would do ourselves good if we take the time to plan and set goals for our lives.

Careful planning puts you ahead in the long run; hurry and scurry puts you further behind. Proverbs 21:5 (MSG)

The Goods on Goal Setting

We hesitate to set goals or reach goals because we fail to see the benefits of goal setting. We experience gratification when a goal is met. The time, energy, effort and consistency spent purposing a goal explodes in pleasure and delight when the goal is realized.

Achieving goals increases energy. Achieving goals drives passion to another level. Achieving goals gives us a sense of confidence. Achieving goals solidifies our personal strengths and willpower. Achieving goals keeps us focused.

> **So let's keep focused on that goal, those of us who want everything God has for us. If any of you have something else in mind, something less than total commitment, God will clear your blurred vision— you'll see it yet! Now that we're on the right track, let's stay on it.** Philippians 3:15-16 (MSG)

Goal setting happens on many levels. The top of the pyramid is the big picture goal. What do we want to accomplish? Next, the goal is separated into manageable steps that will direct us to the goal, the top of the pyramid. From there, our day to day activities will be the stage by which we move up the pyramid.

Galvanizing Goals

The key to goal setting is formulating goals with clarity. I learned this process the hard way. Each year I was required to submit business-related goals. During the planning sessions one year, the department I worked for had a temporary person filling in as manager. This manager declined my submission three times. After the third rejection, I made an appointment with the manager. He taught me the most powerful habit of goal setting. He explained how important the goal setting activity was to my future at the company. This manager showed me how to write S.M.A.R.T. goals.

S = Specific: Goals should be very simple and specific. This is the what and/or why of your goal statement.

M = Measurable: Goals must be measurable. The statement "what gets measured gets done" is applicable here. Mark Sanborn says "You will measure what you treasure."

A goal of losing weight is not measurable. However, the goal statement "I will lose 15 lbs" is measurable.

A = Action-Oriented: The action of the goal statement is how you are going to achieve the goal. This is where other goal setting steps are introduced.

R = Realistic: Goals must be attainable. Goals should be doable but not easy. Goals should make us stretch beyond our comfort zone but within reach. Setting a goal to never buy another pair of shoes is definitely unrealistic. A better goal is limiting shoe purchases to two pairs a month.

T = Time-bound: Goals should have a deadline. The deadline is the when portion of the goal statement. Setting a timeframe motivates us to get started now. If we don't place a date of accomplishment, we never get started or procrastinate.

I always wanted to write a book. I decided that 2007 would be the year that I begin the process to accomplish this dream. I turned the dream into a goal by writing it down. This was my plan:

I am a prolific writer!

Goal: By March 30, 2008, I will publish my first book.

	How	Deadline
1.	Research how to write a book	6/30/07
2.	Decide on topic	7/28/07
3.	Write Rough Outline	8/18//07
4.	Write 1 chapter every 2 weeks	12/30/07
5.	Complete Second Draft	3/15/08
6.	Send to Publisher	3/30/08

This was my initial plan to writing the book that is now in your hands. Writing the goal and attaching deadlines put feet to my goal.

The goal is *Specific*: Writing a book. The goal is *Measurable*: A physical object to handle and hold. The goal is *Action-Oriented*: Steps to follow. The goal is *Realistic*: It's doable within a year's time. The goal is *Time-bound*: March 30, 2008.

Goal Governance

I am a very busy person with many demands on my time. I began to miss my deadlines. I needed someone to keep me accountable. I am very cautious who I share my dreams and aspiration with. You would be wise to do that

47

also. Everyone will not support and encourage you in your dreams. However, you need to find someone who you can trust and keep you focused.

I found that person in my daughter. I was at work lamenting over the fact that I was missing my deadlines. I needed someone to help me. I prayed and asked God to show me someone. He showed me my daughter. I called her and told her I needed her help with my book project. I told her I needed her to call me every Tuesday to remind me of my Thursday's deadlines. I also told her she had my permission to reprimand me when I started slacking off. She laughed! I quickly reminded her that I was still her mother. She agreed. Although I missed the initial deadline for publishing the book, having my daughter to hold me accountable allowed me to realize a goal from my *5-Star Life*.

The scriptures reinforce this principle of having wise counsel around you.

Purposes *and* plans are established by counsel; and [only] with good advice make *or* carry on war. Proverbs 20:18 (AMP)

Refuse good advice and watch your plans fail; take good counsel and watch them succeed. Proverbs 15:22 (MSG)

Quest for Quality

A *5-Star Life* requires focus, planning, and goal-setting.

Write down 5 goals that will move you toward living a *5-Star Life*. These goals do not need to be extravagant. The goals should birth *5-Star* habits that will prepare you for your future.

Select one your goals. Clarify the goal clearly with the S.M.A.R.T. concept

Specific – Define clearly the goal.
Measurable – Place a deadline when the goal will be met.
Action Oriented – What are the steps necessary to achieve the goal.
Realistic – The goal is doable.
Time-bound – Put a deadline when the goal will be met

Repeat this process with the other goals you have written down.

What you do every morning determines what is important to you. Review your goals each morning to keep you focused and passionate about your *5-Star Life*.

Chapter 4

The Principle of Documenting Procedures:
Scripting A 5-Star Life

"For whatsoever things were written aforetime were written for our learning, that we through patience and comfort of the scriptures might have hope."
Romans 15.4

"Good thoughts are no better than good dreams, unless they be executed."
Ralph Waldo Emerson

They're everywhere. Documents. Documents. Documents. You cannot get around it. Documents begin when we are born and end, for us, when we die.

The American Heritage dictionary defines documents as *"A written or printed paper that bears the original, official, or legal form of something and can be used to furnish decisive evidence or information."* Documents are a way of life.

Our birth is documented on a birth certificate. When we die, our death will be documented on a death certificate. A unique identifier for individuals within the United States is documented on a social security card. When we go for medical exams, we begin the documentation process of our health history. Our school years are documented on transcripts. The privilege of driving is documented on a state license. If we choose to marry, we apply for a marriage license. If, unfortunately, the marriage dissolves, it is documented in divorce papers. Our insurance policies are documented contracts. Pay stubs, tax returns, and utility bills are forms of documentation. Photographs document a moment in time. Our newspapers and magazine subscriptions are means of documenting information. Our computers are used as a means of documenting and communicating information. What would the day look like without documents?

Documentation is important for communicating information to others, preserving history, and using as objective evidence to confirm or reject things.

Communicating information is essential to life. Ignorance is not bliss. Documentation helps facilitate the exchange of ideas, thoughts, data, and numbers. Saint Luke chapter one verse sixty three records a situation for the need of scripting. Zachariah, a priest, was stricken with dumbness for his lack to believe the angel's prophetic message of the birth of his son. The appointed time came to name the child. Tradition maintained that the son would be named after the father. However, Zachariah was now operating in full belief and was moved to follow the instruction of the angel in naming the child.

He motioned for a writing tablet, and to everyone's surprise he wrote, "His name is John!" (NLT)

Zachariah used documentation to establish and communicate what was to be.

Documentation allows for history to be preserved. Documentation can be in words or pictures. Have you ever taken the time to reflect back on your history? A nostalgic moment is birth every time I look at the picture of my deceased maternal grandmother. Memories flood my mind of summers spent in the hot summers of Snowhill, North Carolina. Days of picking crops, the candy man, pitch black nights, and cousins galore brings my youthful historic days into my present reality.

Have you every taken a trip through a baby's memory book? Pictures of a baby wrapped in a snuggly pink or blue blanket, the hand and foot prints, the birth certificate, the hospitalization information bracelet, and a lock of hair are types of documents that bellow the birth of a child!

Documentation serves as objective evidence or proof to confirm or reject things. In a court of law, the attorney seeks to reveal evidence that will assure a win. An employer asks for a picture ID and social security card to confirm that a person is who they say they are and that they have the legal right to work. A financial institution asks for identification when cashing a check. The apostle John writes of Jesus Christ as the Son of God. John uses the "I AM" statements of Christ and combines them with the selected signs or miracles of Jesus as objective evidence to confirm who Jesus is:

But these are written, that ye might believe that Jesus is the Christ, the Son of God; and that believing ye might have life through his name. John 20:31 (KJV)

Writing down information gives us advantages. One advantage to jotting things down is that it serves as a reminder. We live in a fast-paced world where we are expected, and conditioned to believe that, multitasking—to do more than one thing at the same time— is effective. I'm getting to the point that if I don't write something down, I forget it. The forgetfulness is not due to dementia. The forgetfulness is caused by the lifestyle we have accepted as normal. By writing things down, the mind is uncluttered and allowed to concentrate on the task at hand. So, I begin my day with my "to do" lists. Documentation jogs my memory. The Holy Scriptures validates this practice.

**Write these commandments that I've given you
today on your hearts. Get them inside of you and
then get them inside your children. Talk about
them wherever you are, sitting at home or walking
in the street; talk about them from the time you
get up in the morning to when you fall into bed at
night. Tie them on your hands and foreheads as a
reminder; inscribe them on the doorposts of your
homes and on your city gates.** Deuteronomy 6:6-9
(MSG)

Not only does writing things down serve as a reminder,
documenting keeps us focused. In chapters two and three,
we discussed writing down our vision and goals. Doing this
brings clarity to our *5-Star Life by Design*. The Bible gives
us insight how this principle works. Joshua had been selected
leader over the mighty nation of Israel. Joshua predecessor,
Moses, had died. Joshua had big shoes to fill! However,
Jehovah God visits Joshua and literally tells him to focus on
the task, not the people.

**This book of the law shall not depart out of thy
mouth; but thou shalt meditate therein day and
night, that thou mayest observe to do according
to all that is written therein: for then thou shalt
make thy way prosperous, and then thou shalt
have good success.** Joshua 1:8

The Hebrew word for mediate is *haw-gaw.* Strong's Greek and Hebrew Dictionary define the Hebrew word *haw-gaw* as:

> *"to* murmur *(in pleasure or anger); by implication to* ponder: *- imagine, meditate, mourn, mutter, roar, sore, speak, study, talk, utter"*

Bishop I.V. Hilliard defines meditation as *"to say over and over again in a repetitious manner until it paints a picture on the canvas of your imagination."*

Documentation benefits us by serving as a commitment, contract, or covenant. Insurance policies, warranties, marriage license, employment agreements spell out what we can expect when we partner with such people or agencies. Even our Heavenly Father is committed to us. And He backs it up with his Word!

And the Lord said to Moses, "Write down these laws that I have given you, for they represent the terms of my covenant with you and with Israel."
Exodus 34:27 (TLB)

Now that we have established the importance and advantages of documentation, how does documentation assist us in living our *5-Star Life by Design*? Joseph J. Tsiakals, Charles A. Cianfrani, and John E. (Jack) West in *ISO9001:200 Explained* writes

> *Documentation forms a basis for understanding the system, communicating its processes and requirements within the organization, describing it to other organizations, and determining the effectiveness of implementation.*

Documentation will do the same for us. Writing things down bring clarity that eliminates the fancy ideas we think are happening. Have you ever thought you were doing something all to find out that you were not accurate in your assessment? My weight loss journey was a rude awakening for me. When I toppled the scales at one hundred fifty pounds, a flash of my sister-in-love's face appeared on the scales. My sister warned me that the weight gain begins at age thirty. Of course, I didn't believe her because I always had a handle on what I ate. Or at least I thought I did. I knew I had to do something quick.

Someone suggested that I begin by logging everything I ate. I smugly stated that I only consume healthy foods such as tuna, celery and carrots! Right! My list ended up with items such as French fries, hamburgers, fried chicken, and M&Ms. Documenting takes away the ambiguity.

Our *5-Star Life by Design* will emerge expeditiously when we permit ourselves to form quality habits. A habit, as defined by the American Heritage dictionary, is *"a recurrent, often unconscious pattern of behavior that is acquired through frequent repetition."* Documenting how we are going to live our *5-Star Life by Design* facilitates habit-forming behaviors. After following a recipe for years, one gets to the place that dependence on the recipe is no longer needed. Like a recipe, writing procedures for our *5-Star Life by Design* will establish a pattern of how we do things, step by step, performed in the same manner to assure that we obtain the desired results every time.

Documenting your *5-Star Life by Design* doesn't have to be complicated but it should follow the 4-Cs of communication: Clear, Concise, Complete and Correct.

Quest for Quality

Documentation is important for communicating information to others, preserving history, and using as objective evidence to confirm or reject things.

Documenting information helps us to remember things, to keep us focus, and to serve as a commitment to ourselves and others.

Documenting information sticks better: We think it, we write it, we see it.

Review your documented Mission/Purpose statement and goals.

Your Mission/Purpose statement and goals will be used as we continue our journey to a **5-Star Life**.

Chapter 5

The Principle of Process Management: Structure For A 5-Star Life

⚜

*"But all things should be done with regard to
decency and propriety and in an orderly fashion."*
1 Corinthians 14:40 (AMP)

*"We need to enjoy the process as well as the results.
We don't enjoy the process because
we have not planned for it.
But, if we plan, we can enjoy the life
that we have crafted."*
Author Unknown

Now that we have our vision/mission statement and our goals and measurement, the next step is to define how we are going to obtain and sustain our *5-Star Life by Design*. The answer: process management.

A process is simply transforming inputs into outputs. You perform processes in some way every day. Let's look at a few examples. Example 1 - Laundry: You have dirty clothes. This is the input. You wash the clothes. This is the process. Clean clothes are the output. Example 2 - Rest: You are tired. This is the input. You go to sleep. This is the process. You wake up refreshed. This is the output. Example 3 - Starvation: You are hungry. You want a baked potato. You get a potato. This is the input. You nuke it in the microwave. This is the process. The potato is cooked. This is the output.

Sound simple? Yes. However, what we are not fully conscious of is the process by which we wash clothes, get rest, or bake a potato. Let's take our laundry example. We simply do not "wash" clothes. It's more complex than what it seems. First, we must consider what materials or equipment we need to wash clothes. Our modern age allows for using a washer and a dryer or we can choose to duplicate grandmother's way of doing it by hand. We also need soap powder or liquid. We may or may not choose to use fabric softener. We need water. We have all we need. Right? Wrong!

How are we going to do laundry? We need to make sure that we know how to use the washer and dryer. That means we may need instructions. What temperature does the fabric require? How much soap powder and fabric softener is needed? What criteria determine cleaned clothes? These are elements in a process.

Process management is determining steps and requirements needed to perform the task the same way every time. I like one author's explanation of process management:

Planning and administering the activities necessary to achieve a high level of performance in a process and identifying opportunities for improving quality operational performance and ultimately customer satisfaction. Author unknown

Identifying the process and related elements removes the ambiguity of experiencing a *5-Star Life by Design*.

Let's take a closer look at the elements of Process Management. Since I live in the leading country for obesity, I will use Weight Loss as an example for creating what the business sector calls a Process Diagram or Turtle Diagram.

(The layout resembles a flatten turtle.) An example of the diagram is included at the end of the chapter.

Who Is Responsible

Every process must have an owner. Clarifying an owner is very important. Naming the process and the owner is vital and is evident by placing this box in the center of the diagram. The owner of the process is responsible for driving and obtaining the stated goals and objectives. The owner has the authority to change the process to improve on its performance. Since we are designing our own individual *5-Star Life by Design*, we are the owner of every process that we create. Our Creator has given us life. He instructs that we be good stewards over that which He has given.

The American Heritage Dictionary defines steward as *"one who manages another's property, finances, or other affairs."* Every one is responsible to manage or design their life. This may be an eye opener for some. How many times have we subconsciously given someone else the ownership of our lives? Our moods, attitudes, and behaviors shift and change depending on how others treat us. I know that was my old way of living.

We can fall into weight gain or debt this way. Whenever one of our credible others or career opportunity frustrate or don't perform to our standards, we fall back on our drug of choice, for example, eating or shopping. We can use our drug of choice to numb us from feeling the emotions erupted from our disappointment or frustration.

My personal drug of choice is shopping. I would get my drug — Ms Credit — and off we went to the mall. Whenever I became emotionally low, I used shopping as my "upper." Like all addicts, shopping worked for a while. During one of my shopping shoot-up sessions in 2003, the Spirit spoke to me. I was challenged to confront my issue of depression. I awoke out of the stupor I created for myself. I set boundaries as to when I could go shopping.

Simply put, giving ownership of your life to someone else will forfeit you truly living a *5-Star Life by Design.*

What Is Expected

The next box is the outputs. This is what we expect out of the process. The outputs are the end result of our work or task, the finished product. It's the Steve Covey's "*Start with the end in mind*" discipline. The benefits of meetings goals are indescribable. Once we meet a goal in one area of our life will affect how we approach another area of our life. We will discuss this aspect in more detail in the next chapter. Let's list some outputs from our Weight Loss Process example.

1. Weight Loss/Control
2. More Energy
3. High Self – Esteem
4. Better Quality of Life

What's Feeding Me

Inputs are the raw materials, components, or ingredients that go into the process and become part of the output. I am a trained computer programmer. One of the foundational truths of programming that was drilled into each student was GIGO-

garbage in, garbage out. This foundational truth is the same with each process. We must be very selective in the raw materials that we allow in our process. Inferior ingredients are everywhere. We must set boundaries to the inputs of the process.

I stated earlier about my shopping experience. I set boundaries as to when I would allow myself to go shopping. One of my inputs was my mood. I determined that I could go shopping only when I was in a good mood. Anytime else was off limits.

Some inputs to our Weight Loss Process example could include:

1. Type of Food
2. Liquids
3. Time
4. Mood

What Am I Working With

Every process uses some type of material, tool, or equipment to get the work accomplished. This box describes the hardware needed for the process. Let's list some items we could use in our Weight Loss Process example.

1. Kitchen. If we are going to cook and store food.
2. Cook Book. Need recipes that are healthy and nutritious.
3. Grocery Store. Where we shop for our food
4. Food Scale. To weigh what we are eating
5. Exercise Equipment. Yes, we need this in some form.

Who's Working With Me

This box lists the competency, skills, and training needed for the process to achieve its goals. I am a firm believer that if this box is deficient or lacking, you can forget about the process entirely. We need proper education and training in order to function at our highest peak. Hosea chapter four verse six says "**My people are destroyed for lack of knowledge.**" How well we see this in our world.

I was speaking at a church one Sunday. I polled the congregation as to who wanted to be rich. Every hand went up. My next question dealt with reading the newspaper.

About seventy five percent of the hands went up. I asked questions on what sections are read first? My final question revealed the essence of Hosea chapter four verse six. Not one hand went up for reading the financial page. We want money but do not want to put forth purposeful effort into the activities that prepare us to get the riches we desire.

Having skilled expertise in a process is a must! Let's list some items in the "With Who" box for our Weight Loss Process example.

1. Nutritionist
2. Physician
3. Exercise Trainer
4. Weight Loss Buddy

Each process listed should have someone that holds us accountable. It is easy to slip into apathy. There was a period in my life when I noticed that my skirts were hugging the hips. I was amazed at how much I weighed when I got on scales. I had to do something now to control the weight or I would be in trouble. I called my baby sister who had successfully lost weight. She was gun ho about her endeavor. My mother told me a story that prompted the call.

My baby sister was chosen as the chairperson for a Women's Day event at her church. The event centered around food. My mother recalled that my sister had made some friendly "enemies" because she wanted all healthy food served. I don't know if my sister won the battle, but my sister won me over. My sister agreed to help me. I had to call her every Sunday evening and give a report of my progress. There were Sundays that I didn't call her. Unfortunately—or fortunately—my sister made contact with me by Tuesday. She kept me on track!

Instructions Included

The How Box determines the methods, procedures, and techniques we will use in our process. I consider this box the second most important. We must systematically detail how we are going to perform activities the same way every time. If we don't define the how, we lose the quality of maintaining a *5-Star Life by Design.*

In frustration, my husband once called me "a *blind man's nightmare.*" My husband was tired of looking for the hair comb every morning. When we discussed the issue, I had to admit he was right. I began my *5-Star Life by Design* in this area by determining to be organized. Did you catch that this is one of my life statements? My husband made a positive impact.

Let's list some "How's" for our Weight Loss Process:

1. Caloric Counter Book
2. Approved diet approach
3. Monthly food planner
4. Exercise Schedule

Gaining Ground

The last box gives us the measurement and assessment with which to gauge how we are performing. Some businesses call this box Key Performance Indicators (KPIs). Each process must have KPIs to gauge how well or not so well we are doing. This box records stated goals for the process. As we stated in an earlier chapter, the goals must be SMART: Specific, Measurable, Attainable, Realistic and Timely.

This box is useful in determining corrective actions needed if we are not meeting our goals. We stated earlier that the owner of the process has the right to change the process to improve on its performance. The box is the feedback loop to signal value added activities that should be continued and non-value added activities that need to be removed.

Items for the With What Key Criteria box for our Weight Loss Process example are:

1. Goal: Weight between 135 – 150 lbs.
2. Scales
3. Yearly physical exams
4. Audits (we will discuss this quality tool in a later chapter)

Would you have guessed that losing weight would be so involved? So does every process we participate in. Think about it? Driving to work is a process. Paying bills is a process. Going to a sporting event or theater is a process.

Going to bed is a process. All of these activities are things we do almost every day. How we process these activities will be the determining factor of whether we live a *5-Star Life by Design* or just let life come at us anyway. The choice is ours

Quest for Quality

Process management brings structure and standardization to a *5-Star Life*.

> Select one of your goals or values and create a process. This is a challenging exercise. I strongly encourage you NOT to skip this portion. Those living a *5-Star Life* have structure and standards. This exercise is necessary to realize your *5-Star Life*. It requires your participation. Try it using the diagram on the next page as a guide. A serious searcher of a *5-Star Life* does what it takes in order to realize what it wants.

The Process Management Structure:

> **Process Owner**: You always!
> **Outputs**: Your expected results.
> **Inputs:** What feeds your process.
> **With What:** The tools, materials, and equipment needed in the process
> **With Who**: What skills, knowledge and competencies are needed to allow the process to yield the

desired results. Name a person or organization that you can tap into for help.

How: List the methods, procedures, and techniques you will employ to work the process.

Key Criteria: What measurement will assess that you are on the right track?

Perform this exercise with your other written goals.

With What? (Materials/Equipment Kitchen Cook Book Exercise Equipment Fool Scale Grocery Store		With Who? (Competence/Skills/ Training) Nutritionist Physician Exercise Trainer Weight Loss Buddy
Inputs (Raw Material) Food Liquids Time Emotions	Process Weight Loss Owner Me	Outputs (Finished Product) Weight Loss/Control High Self Esteem Higher Quality Life More Energy
How? (Method/Procedure/ Technique) Exercise Schedule Monthly Food Planner Caloric Counter Book Approved Diet		With What Key Criteria? (Measurement/Assessment) Scales Yearly Exams Audit

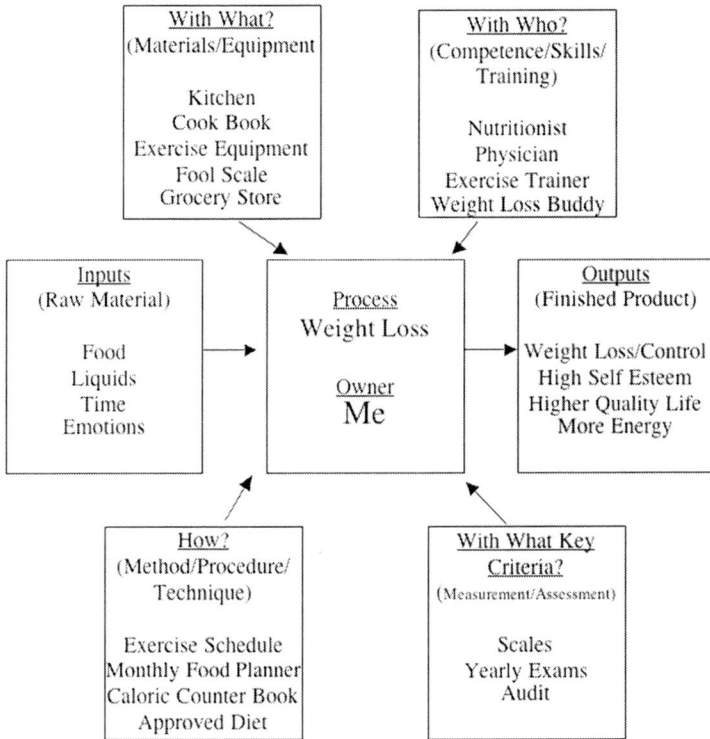

Example of a Turtle (or Process) Diagram

Chapter 6

The Principle of Systems Management: Synchronizing A 5-Star Life

*"And we know that all things work together for
good to them that love God, to them who are the
called according to his purpose."
Romans 8:28*

*"We don't accomplish anything in this world
alone...and whatever happens is the result
of the whole tapestry of one's life and all the
weavings of individual threads from
one to another that creates something.
Sandra Day O'Connor*

L iving a *5-Star Life by Design* requires us to move from silo thinking to systems thinking. Silo thinking in the business world is when individuals, teams, or departments focus on their own goals and objectives and do not consider how their goals and objectives interact or impact other individuals, teams or departments around them. A system is defined as a group of independent but interrelated elements comprising a unified whole. The system can and is usually comprised of subsystems. These subsystems require an infrastructure to manage and coordinate the activities to allow seamless functionality. Systems thinking, unlike silo thinking, require a paradigm shift where we are looking at our entire life and not just one facet of life.

Our bodies are a complex system comprised of subsystems, working together to keep us alive. Our bodies have a circulatory system that transports blood with the help of the heart, arteries and veins. Our bodies have a digestive system that process food with the help of the mouth, esophagus, stomach and intestines. Our bodies have an urinary system that eliminate waste from the body. Our bodies have an immune system, a muscular system, and a skeletal system that keeps us living, moving, and breathing.

Understanding the concept of systems management forces us to understand that making a change in one area could affect another area in the system. Let's take another look at our magnificent bodies. If we become overweight, our circulatory system would be negatively affected by such ailments as high blood sugar and sugar diabetes. Our urinary system may not properly dispel the waste from our bodies that could create such ailments like cancer and kidney failure. In order to enjoy a *5-Star Life by Design*, we must understand the whole of who we are. We are mysterious creatures. We are more than just physical beings. We are triune beings.

And the LORD God formed man *of* the dust of the ground, and breathed into his nostrils the breath of life; and man became a living soul. Genesis 2:7 (KJV)

We are formed from the dust of the ground - physical. We have breath of life – spirit. We became living – soul.

Our spirit makes us conscious toward God. Our soul makes us cognizant towards ourselves. Our bodies connect

79

us to our environment. Apes cannot claim this unique-ness. Fish cannot claim this. The trees or any other part of creation cannot claim this triune mystery that belongs only to mankind.

To benefit from a *5-Star Life by Design*, we must take into consideration the totality of who we are. Looking back at my pre-*5-Star Life by Design*, my goals were concen-trated toward my physical, mental, and social/emotional self. I left out the major part of myself, my spirit man. Dr. I.V. Hilliard affirms "I am a spirit being, encased in a physical body, having a natural experience." Think on the magnitude of that statement. We are more spirit than our physical or natural selves. In proportion, how much do we focus on our spirit self?

The systems management concept challenges us to discover how the several parts of anything fit together to form one integrated whole. I call this system's awareness the *"Five-Ts of Me"*: Touching, Tuning, Targeting, Tasking, and Thriving.

Touching

The American Heritage dictionary defines *touch* as "*a coming together so as to be connected; a situation allowing exchange of ideas or messages.*" We discussed earlier that we are triune beings. It is imperative that we identify and understand how our triad-beings link, relate and reciprocate.

When we recognize that our tri-part beings must touch and relate, we, will experience extraordinary results. Bishop I.V. Hilliard, in his book *Mental Toughness for Success*, explores the complexity and magnitude of the conscience, conscious, and subconscious mind. The soul of mankind is comprised of five elements: the mind, the will, the intellect, the emotion, the imagination. These five elements feed the conscious mind.

The conscious mind makes us aware of our environment. The conscious mind takes a repetitious act or an emotional significant event and files the experience into the subconscious mind.

The subconscious mind allows us to perform acts in which we may not be fully aware of. We can consider this a sort of 'autopilot" response. For example, have you driven to work and could not remember how you arrived? Our subconscious mind was given information on the consistent way in which we drive to work. At some point, our subconscious or "autopilot" took control, releasing the conscious mind to concentrate on something else.

The conscience mind is a repository of what we believe is right or wrong. Our behaviors are formed by what we have deposited into our conscience. Observing the behaviors of someone alert us to that person's belief system or conscience. Our three-facet mind serves as a model of how information, ideas, and messages touch and relate in a system.

Tuning

Tuning implies how we harmonize with the different processes. Systems management requires us to appreciate how the many pieces and parts of our lives synthesize to create our **5-Star Life by Design.** We begin to discover that when we apply a process to one area of our lives, we start to see where other areas of our lives need improving and fine tuning. Agreement is a powerful force. When individuals lay aside personal agendas and focus on how their skills, knowledge and abilities harmonizes with others to complete a project, great things happen. Matthew chapter 18 verse 19 confirms the power of agreement:

> **Again I tell you, if two of you on earth agree (harmonize together, make a symphony together) about whatever [anything and everything] they may ask, it will come to pass *and* be done for them by My Father in heaven.** (AMP)

Let's turn our attention to the operation of a car. A car has many complex and detailed processes that work together to make the car run. A deficiency in one area, like gas, will halt the progress of the purpose of the car. It doesn't matter how sparkling and sleek the car is. Without gas, the car is going nowhere!

Have you ever heard a choir singing in an octave different than the music accompaniment? As a Pastor's wife, I've had the displeasure of experiencing this on many occasions. The combination makes a 3 minute presentation seem like 30 minutes. Tuning is important!

Targeting

The basis of a *5-Star Life by Design* is to reach a desired goal. We are aiming at something. Systems management direct our focus on the goals we have established. A *5-Star Life by Design* determines what needs to be accomplished or achieved. Systems management dictates that every process we put in place will be aimed at achieving common objectives. Lest we forget, the objective is experiencing a **5-Star Life!**

Targeting forces us to focus on the goal. Systems management is useless if the goal is forgotten. Lack of focus is the reason we miss the target. The apostle Paul speaks of his untiring focus for his life in Philippians chapter three verses

thirteen and fourteen:

> **Brethren, I count not myself to have appre-
> hended: but *this* one thing *I do*, forgetting those
> things which are behind, and reaching forth unto
> those things which are before, I press toward the
> mark for the prize of the high calling of God in
> Christ Jesus.**

Paul mentions focusing on the "one" thing. To realize

our goal, we must also target our energy, time, and effort on

our *5-Star Life by Design*. This may sound selfish to some.

It isn't. Targeting allows us to be consciously (see Touching)

aware of the activities that derail and distract us. Targeting

makes us responsible for the results of our lives. Targeting

makes us look for friends that, in the words of Mike Murdock,

feed, fuel and fertilize our efforts. Targeting compels us to

qualify every thing we do to ensure that every effort move us

toward our *5-Star Life by Design*.

Tasking

Tasking identifies how specific activities will operate. It is the 1-2-3, step by step outline of the work required to reach a desired end. Tasking, by far, is the most difficult to implement but the most crucial. Without tasking, the other four Ts lack the energy and force to bring our *5-Star Life by Design* to fruition.

A computer carries within its operating system the instructions or tasks required for the computer to operate at its maximum capacity. When the return key is pressed, instructions are sent to the operating system to advance to the next line. When the space bar is press, instructions are sent to the operating system to forward advance. Imagine the frustration we experience if, when we pressed the enter key, the computer did something other than advance to the next line.

Joshua chapter one through chapter six describes an amazing feat. When Joshua was fighting his first battle, Jehovah God gave him explicit tasks to follow for conquering the walled city of Jericho. Instructions were given to Joshua, to the Israelis, to the priests, and to Rahab, the harlot of Jericho. Everyone executed their instructions. The end result was the conquest of Jericho. Tasking our *5-Star Life by Design* insists that we identify the necessary instructions so that we can, like the computer and like Joshua's conquest of Jericho, rely on predetermined results. This is no small feat. But the results are worth the investment.

Thriving

The American Heritage Dictionary defines thrive as *"to make steady progress; prosper; to grow vigorously; flourish."* Thriving is where we evaluate the system to make improvements. A *5-Star Life by Design* always look to raise the standards to a more desirable, excellent, efficient and effective way of doing things. Thriving sharpens the 5-cyclinder process toward reaching our *5-Star Life by Design*!

Continuous improvement's philosophy implies that making small improvements to processes overtime can yield amazing results. The results can be the difference between receiving the bronze metal or the gold metal.

The woman depicted in Proverbs chapter thirty one is a prime example of systems management. This wife, mother, and entrepreneur managed her life to the point where she is considered priceless.

"Who can find a virtuous woman? for her price is far above rubies." Proverbs 31:10

This phenomenal woman successfully managed her 5-Star life. Her bibliography reveals that she operated at the highest level of her "5-Ts". At home, her husband, children and servants are well taken care of. The activities of feeding, clothing, and providing are a direct reflection of achieving a system where goals are met through open and effective communication channels. This model of excellence is demonstrated in her business affairs. She is keenly aware of real estate transactions and interaction with suppliers and buyers that makes her a savvy business woman. She balances her system by reaching and helping the poor and needy which causes her to touch all aspects of reality. She indeed has cultivated a wise and noble character.

Businesses survive and thrive by consciously planning, organizing, coordinating, communicating, implementing and controlling activities that they believe will give them a competitive edge. These activities are crucial if a business desires to contend in the global economy and profit. A *5-Star Life by Design* requires the same tenacity, intensity and energy of touching, tuning, targeting, tasking, and thriving.

May God himself, the God who makes everything holy and whole, make you holy and whole, put you together—spirit, soul, and body—and keep you fit for the coming of our Master, Jesus Christ. 1 Thessalonians 5:23 (MSG)

We were created holy and whole. Strong's Greek & Hebrew dictionary defines whole as *"complete and perfectly sound in every part to the conclusion of an act, state or result."* Living a *5-Star Life by Design* is our authentic right. We were created and purposed for it. It's up to us to desire it, choose it, design it, and manage it!

Quest for Quality

Systems management is a compilation of the processes in a *5-Star Life*.

Review the process structures you created in the previous chapter.

Systems management requires that the processes created fit together to form an integrated whole. The system MUST work together to move towards a *5-Star Life*. Review the processes you documented. Evaluate if the processes are:

Touching: How do the processes connect?

Tuning: Are the processes in harmony? The output from one process should successfully feed the input into another process.

Targeting: Are the processes aligned to reach the purpose of a *5-Star Life*?

Tasking: Are all processes defined to specify the activity to perform to realize a *5-Star Life*?

Thriving: Is the system running at optimum capacity to produce a *5-Star Life*?

Refine each process to ensure that all processes are moving toward accomplishing and achieving the goals you have defined.

Chapter 7

The Principle of Internal Audits: Scrutinizing a 5-Star Life

⚜

"I the LORD search the heart, I try the reins,
even to give every man according to his ways, and
according to the fruit of his doings."
Jeremiah 17.10

"It is the quality of our work which will
please God and not the quantity."
Mahatma Gandhi

I confess. I hate stepping on weigh scales. It doesn't matter if I did everything "right"—eat nutritious, exercised three times a week, consumed 8-8oz glasses of water—I just panic. However, every Sunday morning, I brace myself, step on the scales, and watch the number display.

I don't believe anyone enjoys being under the microscope. Human nature does not receive rejection well. We all want things to go our way. We crave for everything to fall in place whether we have worked for it or not. It's just the way we are wired.

Living a *5-Star Life by Design*, unfortunately, mandates that we undergo scrutiny to gauge whether or not we are living up to what we have designed for our lives. This activity in the business world is called auditing. Auditing is to undergo thorough scrutiny to assess that current practices meet defined requirements.

We perform audits in many areas of our lives. We balance our checkbooks to make sure we have sufficient funds in our account. We analyze our bank and credit card statements for accuracy. Every April, American citizens are required to file tax returns so that the government can audit and analyze our income. We go to the doctor and dentist for examinations. Are these activities fun? No! Are they necessary? Yes. A wise person will implement the practice of self-audits.

But let every person carefully scrutinize *and* examine *and* test his own conduct *and* his own work. **He can then have the personal satisfaction *and* joy of doing something commendable [in itself alone] without [resorting to] boastful comparison with his neighbor.** Galatians 6:4 (AMP)

Auditing is a fact-finding activity. Auditing is not intended to be a fault finding blame game. The goal of auditing is to analyze processes and procedure to assure compliance (*to act in accordance with*) to written documentation or specifications.

Audit practices originated from the financial world where businesses would check records for accuracy. The audit would reveal if financial practices were followed and reveal the strength of a company.

In recent years, auditing has crossed over into functional areas such as quality, environmental and safety. The purpose, however, is the same: to validate if standard practices are followed and reveal the strength of operations.

Gary Ryan Blair in his article *Thou Shalt Inspect What Thy Expect* gives credence to the auditing process. Mr. Blair acknowledges a dual purpose to auditing or inspection:

"First, inspection tells you where you are in relation to where you want to be. Second, it tells you how you're doing in the process of pursuing your goals."

Our efforts of living a *5-Star Life by Design* are wasted if we do not build in the activity to audit or inspect where we are with our vision, goals and process systems. Auditing acknowledges that our actions align to our words: I do what I say and say what I do!

Our human psyche can convince us that we are doing something when in reality we are not. I remember the time I use to "boast" that I did not waste time watching TV. One evening, the Holy Spirit revealed "me" to me. I had made plans to accomplish three things on a particular evening. When I returned home from work, while changing clothes, a television program caught my attention. Two hours later the show ended. As I complained how late it was, the Holy Spirit's small gentle voice echoed my false "boastings". I was arrested.

How subtle we deceive ourselves. Deception occurs when we allow our mental maps to persuade us that we are OK. We are bamboozled by our behavior without questioning or examining the effects that our actions bring into being. To avoid fraudulent behavior, auditing takes a nonbiased approach to assure we are truly living out the *5-Star Life* that we designed.

The use of documents, discussed in an earlier chapter, becomes an input to the auditing process. The audit identifies the plans of what we are supposed to do. An audit cannot be conducted if there is no plan or criteria to match against evidence. The audit process makes observations to determine what is actually happening. The audit should look for objective evidence or facts to support what is actually happening. Documented evidence is much stronger than verbal validation. Let's go back to our weight scenario as an example. During the audit, we can "say" that we weigh ourselves once a week. However, if we produced a chart showing the date and what we weighed, the objective evidence leaves no room for subjective analysis from the auditor.

95

The end result of the audit process actualizes several advantages in assisting us to living out our *5-Star Life by Design*. These advantages are the 4-As: Achievements, Aberrations, Assimilations and Advancements.

The first advantage is to actualize *achievement* of agreed upon requirements. The evidence collected by the auditor will confirm that we are realizing the goals that we have set out in living our *5-Star Life by Design*. We are on track, staying focus, and moving toward our goals. These are the "atta boy" kudos that we want to hear.

> **His master commended him: 'Good work! You did your job well. From now on be my partner.'**
> Matthew 25.23 (MSG)

The second advantage is to reveal any *aberrations* or deviations from the proper or expected course. These findings or non-conformances are sometimes hard to accept. However, the discoveries are necessary to help up correct what we are doing so that we can reach and live out what we have designed. David, the great psalmist, says it well for us in Psalm one hundred thirty ninth division and verses twenty three and twenty four:

Investigate my life, O God, find out everything about me; Cross-examine and test me, get a clear picture of what I'm about; See for yourself whether I've done anything wrong—(MSG)

Assimilation is the third advantage for auditing. Assimilating means to take in and incorporate any best practices that will help us meet our goals. The auditor is a second pair of eyes that can objectively suggest implementing other practices to aid us in our quest to a *5-Star Life by Design.* The Apostle Paul gives us affirmation in this practice when he wrote the people of Thessalonica. He instructs them to implement everything that is good.

But examine everything carefully; hold fast to that which is good; 1 Thessalonians 5:21(NASU)

The last advantage to auditing is *advancement.* The audit results will clearly and concisely report the conformances and the non-conformances from the evidence collected. The value of discovering the non-conformances is to put a plan in place to correct what should be happening so that what we have designed for our *5-Star Life by Design* will materialize. So, we will not be hard pressed when the non conformances are revealed. We will take it as an opportunity to hone our plans for forward mobility. The goal of living a *5-Star Life by Design* is to always advance to a more desirable state.

But we all, with open face beholding as in a glass the glory of the Lord, are changed into the same image from glory to glory, *even* **as by the Spirit of the Lord.** 2 Corinthians 3.18

We will discuss implementing corrective actions in the next chapter.

So far we have discussed what an audit is and the advantages obtained by auditing. This last section will instruct us on how to set up our audits to evaluate our *5-Star Life by Design*.

First, we need to identify someone to conduct the audit. One of the principles of auditing is that an auditor cannot audit their own work. That means you cannot audit yourself. The person you choose should be someone who cares about you. David, the great psalmist, used this principle and asked his Heavenly Father to audit him.

GOD, investigate my life; get all the facts first-hand. I'm an open book to you; even from a distance, you know what I'm thinking. You know when I leave and when I get back; I'm never out of your sight. You know everything I'm going to say before I start the first sentence. Psalm 139.1-4 (MSG)

The person you choose should be someone who will be honest and truthful about the discovery process. The auditor should "speak the truth in love" so that the event will yield value to your life. Look around you. There are many people to assist you in this activity. I find that my children are the best auditors for me. Sometimes I think they enjoy it too much! I also get another perspective on life because they are younger. I also have friends my age who I have asked to audit my life. One girlfriend gives it to me straight. But, that's what I need.

Second, we must define what we want the audit to cover. Since we have documented our *5-Star Life by Design,* we can have the audit cover one process or the entire system. We should set up a schedule to determine the intervals by which we undergo audits.

Third, we must resolve that we will fix problems or non-conformities that are revealed during the audits. If we are not willing to do this, the audit is useless.

The last step is that we will undergo a verification process by which the auditor have objective evidence that we have fixed or solved the problems or nonconformities that were discovered.

Let's plan the audit process for our *5-Star Life by Design*!

Quest for Quality

Auditing is a fact finding activity. Auditing is not intended to be a fault finding, blame game

How do you handle constructive criticism?

What preparations can you make to adjust your mental map to receive criticism positively instead of negatively?

One of the principles of auditing is that an auditor cannot audit their own work.

List some people who you would be comfortable auditing your 5-Star Life.
Why did you select these people?
Could these people audit your entire system or just certain processes? Why?

Three months from the day you implement a process:

Schedule an audit of this process
Select an auditor
Prepare your documentation:
    Vision/Mission statement
    Process diagram
    Objective evidence for the process being audited

Chapter 8

The Principle of Corrective Actions: Sharpening A 5-Star Life

∽✖✎

"The whole Bible was given to us by inspiration
from God and is useful to teach us what is true and
to make us realize what is wrong in our lives; it
straightens us out and helps us do what is right."
2 Timothy 3.16 (TLB)

"In the middle of every difficulty lies opportunity."
Albert Einstein

I wake up in my Northeast Ohio bed on Friday, March 7. The sun is shining. I hum a favorite song as I shimmy my way to the bathroom to prepare for the day. I love white. I pick out my favorite summer white dress to wear to work. My hair falls into place. My make-up is applied perfectly. My husband gets up to start breakfast. The drive to work catches all green lights. My work day is uneventful. The drive home, again, catches all green lights. The plan for the evening is to engage in a romantic dinner with Husband at one of our favorite spots. As I lay in bed that evening I exclaimed "just perfect!"

Reality check

The weather report for Friday March 7 is 3-9 inches of snow accumulating before the day end. I dread getting up because I really don't want to go to work. I don't wear white because I work in a manufacturing plant. I haven't visited my hairstylist in two weeks. No comment on how my make-up looks. Husband is snoring lightly and I'm sure his dreams do not consist of getting up with me at 5am in the morning. There are five lights on my normal route to work. I catch three red lights. Oh My! I forget I'm working at another plant today. Of the two traffic lights on my route, I catch one red light. I notice the snow starting to fall around 11am. The normal fifteen minute drive home turns out to be a one hour drive. I'm thankful for good tires and four-wheel drive! The romantic dinner consists of Penn Station sandwiches that Husband brings home. I fall asleep on the couch thanking God that I made it through another day.

We all have aspirations of what our lives should be. The reason of Living our *5-Star Life by Design* is to have our aspirations manifest. Yet the actions required to catapult us to our *5-Star Life by Design* does not always match up with what we have planned and documented.

In the last chapter we talked about auditing our *5-Star Life by Design* to confirm that we are carrying out what we have agreed to do. More times than not, we are hit with areas in which we need to correct.

Not too many people enjoy correction. Correction is discipline designed to restore. My mother was the godly disciplinarian in the home. If one of her children wanted to go somewhere, Mother would assign another sibling to tag along for good measure. I was matched up with Sister #2. Sister #2 and I are one and one fourth years apart from each other. We were both athletic. I was ordinary. My sister, on the other hand, was adventurous, self-confident and didn't take much from anyone. She was my idol and had great influence over me. Needless to say, we found ourselves in mischievous situations which Mother decided needed correcting. Mother's usual form of discipline was sending us to our rooms for a specified amount of time.

My sister would mourn and go through grief because she liked her freedom. I, on the other hand, loved it. I am a natural loner who enjoys reading books. My so-called punishments became "make-shift" vacation spots for me. During one of my "make-shift vacations," I didn't hear Mother approaching the room. There she observed me lying on my back, my feet crossed in the air, enraptured with my book! She opened her mouth to tell me that her choice of punishment for me wasn't punishment. I was enjoying it too much. Mother wisely chose to continue to execute "time-out" for my sister; but I was given the rod that "didn't spoil the child".

The world has conditioned us to see correction as failure. The grading system in elementary school was a rude awakening in perfection. I obsessed over grades. I wanted a "A". And "A+" was even better. The teacher's big bright red "A+" confirmed that I was all that and a bag of chips. If I received anything lower or my classmates received a higher grade than me, I felt like a failure. So often we stop trying to reach goals because we do not want to feel like failures. John Maxwell has authored an excellent book in how to relate to failure that I recommend for reading. *Failing Forward: turning mistakes into stepping stones for success* presents the case that viewing failure correctly actually assist us in moving forward. Adding failure as a part of the process frees us to risk more and live more. Mr. Maxwell encapsulates embracing failure with fifteen elements:

1. Realize there is one major difference between average people and achieving people
2. Learn a new definition of failure
3. Remove the "you" from failure
4. Take action and reduce your fear
5. Change your response to failure by accepting responsibility
6. Don't let the failure from outside get inside you
7. Say good-bye to yesterday
8. Change yourself, and your world changes
9. Get over yourself and start giving yourself

10. Find the benefits in every bad experience
11. If at first you do succeed, try something harder
12. Learn from a bad experience and make it a good experience
13. Work on the weakness that weakens you
14. Understand there's not much difference between failure and success
15. Get up, get over it, get going.

Correction is a part of life. We have progressed from eyeglasses to corrective lens to laser eye surgery to correct poor sight. There is hip replacement to correct and remove pain and restore mobility. Pacemakers help correct abnormal heart rhythm. With such wonderful advancement in medical technology, we can say that there are benefits to correction.

First, correction is necessary for growth and maturing. We tend to think discipline is needed just for the young. The Living Translation of Proverbs chapter twenty three verse thirteen says **"Don't fail to correct your children; discipline won't hurt them!"** If we dive deeper in application, each season we enter into brings about "childish" behaviors. Reflect back at a time when you embarked on a new job for a new company. Did you know everything? Probably not. You had to submit to another person's help to introduce you to the company, the culture, and the characters. Knowing the location of the bathroom was relevant information.

Second, correction signals relationship. Proverbs chapter three verse twelve states **"For whom the Lord loves He corrects, even as a father corrects the son in whom he delights"** (AMP). The American Heritage Dictionary defines the root word *relate* as "t*o establish or demonstrate a connection between."* As I was growing up, I thought my parents where down-right mean. My siblings and I were raised by strict parents who did not believe in allowing children to run wild. We had to report every where we went. We could not visit, go to a party, or spend the night anywhere if our parents did not know the parents of our friends. Many days I wanted to be a part of a family that lived down the street. We were in church every Sunday. Missing church meant that all activities outside of school were off limits for the following week. We had to be in the house before the street lights came on. And everybody in the block knew it.

My older sister and I decided one Wednesday evening to invite two boys over while our parents were at a church function. As Dad walked in the back door, he boomed "Who's in my house?" Before we could make the introductions, Daddy said "wait right here while I go get my gun!" My sister and I were horrified. Our friends high-tailed it out the front door. They did not wait around to hear us explain that Dad was just playing. The next day in school was torture. As we made our way into our Junior High School, it was noised abroad not to visit the Butler sisters—You may end up dead. My sister and I told Dad what happened that day. Dad chuckled. We saw no humor it.

Looking back I now know that my parents were looking out after our own best interest. The motive was that we were extensions of them. Plenty of days my siblings and I heard Mother say that she's didn't have time to be our friend, but our parent—we'll be friends when you are grown. I'm glad my parents were parents. Today I have a great relationship with them.

Relationships extend beyond people. If we take a quick inventory, we can come up with many relationships. I relate to my company, to my church, to my community. I relate to the function of my career path. I relate to my *5-Star Life by Design* and the dreams and goals I have established to get me there. I relate to my entrepreneurial endeavors. Even as I write this paragraph, I'm relating to this book, this chapter, and to these words. Correction, at any level, occurs in every relationship.

Third, correction helps control our behavior. Proverbs chapter sixteen verse thirty two states **"Moderation is better than muscle, self control-better than political power"** (MSG). You can agree with me that our world has become one of no restraint. We have become a society where there seems to be no self-discipline. Quick fixes for the things we desire and lust after is revealed in the crimes that are sending our children to prison. Child abuse cases are heard every day. We have unethical practices and behaviors in corporations that lead to public distrust. Politicians are being voted out of office because of inappropriate actions.

The benefit of corrective actions is revealed in our self-discipline in obtaining our dreams. I chuckle as I write this. I have just completed my forty-day fast for the Lent season.

I gave up Pepsi, sweets, and shopping. It was a fight to the finish to resist the temptation to give in and indulge. Yet, I can say in the words of Hebrews chapter twelve verse eleven

No discipline is enjoyable while it is happening—it is painful! But afterward there will be a quiet harvest of right living for those who are trained in this way. (NLT).

Now that we understand the benefits of correction, let apply the Correction Action concept to our *5-Star Life by Design*.

Cast The Team

As we begin the process of correcting the deficiencies in our *5-Star Life by Design*, it is crucial to implore the help of those who support us and want to see us succeed. We are the main character in our *5-Star Life by Design*. Life, though, is more fulfilling when we have supporting characters that encourage and enrich us. One character plays are entertaining. More actors engaged in a play, however, yields a more diverse and entertaining performance.

Responsible friends and support characters bring different viewpoints. Be careful not to fall into the trap of two of my favorite commercials. The first commercial involves a man that says "dude" in every situation he finds himself in. The second commercial includes two famous basketball players. The younger player finally succeeds, after many attempts, in getting into the network of an older player that he admired. The younger player, unfortunately, realizes that the older player is void of any useful conversation.

When casting our team to help us resolve problems, we must consider what people bring to the table. We find the best resources in the most unlikely people. Recruit individuals beyond your normal boundaries. Soliciting people with differing backgrounds will avoid the behavior of "group think" (people who bring no diversity to a situation). These viewpoints are needed to help discover the root problem that caused the nonconformities and discover a remedy to fix and alleviate the problem. Remember Proverbs chapter eleven verse fourteen:

Without good direction, people lose their way; the more wise counsel you follow, the better your chances (MSG).

The team you cast to help you through the corrective action process must be permitted to share their insight. We must give them permission to share. As I write this I'm listening to a local news channel. A young man, not wanting to be identified, is sharing his story of the guilt and shame he feels for not having a job. His family believes he is going to work everyday. Instead, he makes daily visits to the unemployment center for help in securing a job. The next news segment showed the newscaster speaking with a radio personality. As the newscaster is sharing her thoughts of how wonderful and sentimental the prior segment was, the radio personality blasts the television newscaster for exploiting the young man. The radio personality passionately stated that what the news station should have done was taken the young man's name and helped him find a job. Instead of bickering, the television newscaster politely agreed and gave out the television station's telephone number to correct the situation.

Objectives setting

An objective is something worked toward or striven for. The selected team must understand what needs to be accomplished during their time together. Establishing the ground rules help keep the team focused and productive in solving the problem.

Root Cause Analysis

Root cause analysis is, by far, the most tedious part of the process. Root cause analysis does what the name implies. We can so easily be misled by identifying the symptoms and miss discovering the true problem.

One of my favorite problem solving tools is called the 5-Whys. The tool works by stating the problem and drilling down to discover the root cause by asking "why." The 5-Why tool works much like the curiosity of a child. Children naturally have the ability to execute this concept. They ask questions about everything. A child is told "go wash your hands." The child asks "Why?" The child is told "so that your hands will be clean." The child asks "Why?" The child is told "so that your hands won't carry germs." The child asks "why?" The child is told "so you don't get sick." The child asks "Why?" The child is told "so that you don't miss school." Some where along the line we were conditioned to stop asking questions!

Recommending Corrective Actions

Once the problem has been discovered, the next task is to resolve and eliminate the problem. This step can be an easy fix or a very difficult journey. Just as it was important to get to the root cause of a problem and not the symptom, recommending corrective actions must be just as rigorous. Take a lesson from the dandelions—those yellow critters that spot our lawns every spring through fall. We can choose between two solutions to get rid of dandelions. First, we can select an evening to pluck them up. The lawn would look beautiful for a few days. In a couple of days, however, patches of yellow will pop up again. We only resolved the problem for a few days. The second choice is to treat the lawn so that the dandelions will die. This second choice is a much better solution to implement.

Brainstorming sessions are useful in recommending corrective actions. Brainstorming is when a group of people come together for the purpose of generating ideas to solve a problem. The beauty of brainstorming is that no suggestion is a bad one. After a time limit has been exhausted, the team eliminates the ideas that would not produce the desired results. The session should yield ideas that will eliminate the nonconformity.

The scriptures are filled with wonderful corrective actions for the problems of life we face. Here are a few of my favorite ones:

> **This I recall to my mind, therefore have I hope. It is of the LORD'S mercies that we are not consumed, because his compassions fail not. They are new every morning: great is thy faithfulness.** Lamentations 3.21-23

> **Be strong, courageous, and firm; fear not nor be in terror before them, for it is the Lord your God Who goes with you; He will not fail you or forsake you.** Deuteronomy 31.6 (AMP)

> **A man's mind plans his way, but the Lord directs his steps and makes them sure.** Proverbs 16.9 (AMP)

> **If we confess our sins, he is faithful and just to forgive us our sins, and to cleanse us from all unrighteousness.** 1 John 1.9

> **Always remember that it is the LORD your God who gives you power to become rich, and he does it to fulfill the covenant he made with your ancestors.** Deuteronomy 8.18 (NLT)

Executing Corrective Actions

Once solutions have been decided on, the solutions must be implemented. If we are to see any results in our *5-Star Life by Design*, we must be willing to discipline ourselves in putting into practice that which we have agreed would eliminate the problems that are halting us from reaching our goals. The result of coming up with solutions is to implement them. James chapter four verse seven reads **"Faith without works is dead."** My interpretation of this verse is "I must work out what I wish about."

Confirmation of Effectiveness

It is a waste of time, money and energy to perform audits and execute corrective actions if there is not a way to determine if the corrective actions eliminated the problem. No need to worry, though. Living our *5-Star Life by Design* mandates that we include this step to move us positively along our journey.

119

Confirming the effectiveness of our solutions means to check, adjust, or determine by comparison with a standard. This implies looking at information that caused the problem and comparing that information against the results seen after executing corrective actions. Confirming effectiveness can take place immediately or a set time period in the future. My experience and best time frame to measure effectiveness is three months from the time corrective actions have been completely executed.

Habits are not easily adopted. Steve Covey defines habit as "the intersection of knowledge, skill, and desire." Knowledge is easily obtained as to the "why" something needs to happen. The skill is learned as to "how" to implement the "why." Desire, "the motivation", to execute the "how" that is launched from the "why" comes from within. I *know* that exercise is good for me. I have acquired the *skill* in working the tread mill that increases my cardiovascular and the weights that build up my muscles. My fight comes in the arena of desire. Excuses such as "I don't have time today," or "I'm too tired" are constant battles of my flesh. Yet, I feel so much better when I fight through the excuses and do what I need to do. This is the problem with New Year's resolution. We start out on fire but soon the fire turns into a fading flame. Confirming effectiveness too early may not allow us to solidify the behaviors needed to propel us closer to our *5-Star Life by Design.*

Thank You

After the above steps are completed, the last and exciting step is to celebrate! Having a thankful attitude toward those who want the best for you provides a conduit in which your supporters are honored to help you. No one likes or wants to be around a person who is not appreciative. Thankless people are draining, damaging and deadening. That is not us, though. We are on our way to living a *5-Star Life by Design.* There is no room for ungratefulness. A *5-Star Life by Design* believes in sowing and reaping. Where we sow gratitude, gratitude comes back to us. Where we sow appreciation, appreciation comes back to us. Where we sow thankfulness, thankfulness comes back to us. So, where we celebrate others, others will celebrate us.

Corrective Action Illustrated

Joshua chapter seven illustrates the seven principles of correction action. The children of Israel had just won an incredible battle at Jericho. Israel's next exploit was a city named Ai (pronounced A-I) which had a few people. The army of Israel felt it would be an easy win. It wasn't. Israel suffered a great loss. Joshua and the elders *(casting the team)* came together to find out what happened *(objective setting)*. Joshua and the team tore their clothes and lay prostrate to entreated Jehovah God for answers. The Lord shared with Joshua that someone disobeyed the instructions that was given for the battle of Jericho. Early one morning, beginning with verse sixteen, each of the twelve tribes were brought before Joshua until one tribe was taken, Judah. Joshua drilled down and ask 'Why Judah?" The answer: because of the family of Zarhites. Joshua asked "Why the family of

Zarhites?" The answer: because of the household of Zabdi. Again, Joshua asked "Why the household of Zabdi?" The answer: because of the man Achan. When Joshua asked Achan why he was chosen, Achan acknowledged his disobedience by taking spoils of the city and hiding it in his tent (*root cause analysis*).

The Lord had shared with Joshua that if Israel wanted His presence back, the issue must be destroyed (*recommending corrective action*). Joshua and the entire Israeli camp, according to verses twenty four and twenty five, destroyed the cause of the problem *(executing corrective actions)*.

The next battle for the Israeli army was to go against Ai again. The Lord's instructions guaranteed victory. They did (*confirmation of effectiveness*)! And the people were instructed to keep the spoils (*thank you*).

Living our *5-Star Life by Design* will not always guarantee that we practice what we print. We are humans and are subject to failure. Failure, however, does not mean finality. We have a choice: To correct or reject.

We will end this chapter with a wise statement from Ralph Waldo Emerson:

> *Finish everyday and be done with it. You have done what you could; some blunders and absurdities crept it; forget them as soon as you can. Tomorrow is a new day; you shall begin it serenely and with too high a spirit to be encumbered with your old nonsense.*

Quest for Quality

Corrective Actions provides an opportunity to grow, mature, and sharpen our behavior.

Take an area of your 5-Star Life that needs improving. Walk through the seven steps of Corrective Actions and document all activities (corrective action and verification of effectiveness).

Chapter 9

The Principle of Cost of Quality: Securing A 5-Star Life

⁂

"For God so greatly loved and dearly prized the world that He [even] gave up His only begotten (unique) Son..."
John 3.16a (AMP)

"How we spend our days is, of course, how we spend our lives."
Annie Dillard

E verything costs! Nothing in life is free. There is a price for every pursuit, every passion, and every project we undertake in this life. Everyday that we are blessed to live will require a deposit of some type of payment that will come to fruition in our future. The American heritage dictionary defines cost as the *"expenditure of something, such as time or labor, necessary for the attainment of a goal."*

Labor Payment

Adam, the first man created, was placed in a beautiful garden named Eden. Adam did not have to plant trees. The trees were already there. Adam did not have to make animals. The animals were already there. Yet, when God placed Adam in the garden, God instructed Adam to dress the garden. The Interlinear Bible says **"to work it and to keep it.** (Genesis 2.15). Adam's price to stay in the garden of Eden was an energy cost.

Creativity Payment

Adam had another cost to cough up. God instructed Adam to name the many animals that He created. Genesis chapter 2 verse 19, the Interlinear Bible says

And Jehovah God formed every animal of the field, and every bird of the heavens out of the ground. And He brought them to the man to see what he would call it. And all which the man might call it, each living soul, that was its name. And the man called names to all the cattle, and the bird of the heavens, and every animal of the field.

Adam was called upon to pay the price of creativity to name the giraffes, the monkeys, the elephants, the serpents, the dolphins, the whales, and every creeping thing in the animal kingdom.

Time Payment

Joseph was the favorite son of Israel and Rachel. He was a dreamer. Joseph's visions were clear. His parents and his siblings would bow down to him. Unfortunately, his brothers did not take kind to Joseph's dreams. Joseph's brothers sold him into slavery. Joseph ends up as a slave to Potipher. Jehovah God's favor on Joseph causes Potipher to elevate Joseph to number one in the household. Sexual desires from Potipher's wife, but God-conscious morals from Joseph, resulted in Joseph being placed in prison. Joseph's integrity and ethics propelled him to promotion even in prison. Joseph's time payment in prison did not stop his purpose from protruding. Joseph's gift of dreams precisely interpreted the fate of two of the King's servants. When the king himself was plagued by a disturbing dream, Joseph's name was brought before the king. Joseph's gift was not abated by the thirteen-year time payment that, to the flesh and impatience of humankind, may appear to have been unfair and a waste of time. Joseph's accurate interpretation of the King's dream landed him a position of second in command in the great land of Egypt.

Money Payment

Hosea, the prophet, was commanded by Jehovah God to marry a harlot, Gomer. Gomer ended up on the slave block because of her sexual promiscuity. Hosea used his hard-earned money to purchase back his adulterous wife.

The Sanhedrin counsel paid Judas 30 pieces of silver for betraying Jesus the Christ.

Cost of Quality

In the quality field, the cost of quality is the price a company pays to ensure that its services or products are made right the first time or the amount of money a company loses because of inferior quality. A payment is made in either way. When the payment is made upfront, a company's name is propelled to a prominent position in the industry. The company's reputation causes current and prospective customers to seek the service or product of the company. When a company's quality is plagued with persistent problems and unreliable functionality, the company pays with recall costs, loss of sales, and customer defection to a competitor.

Another way we can interpret cost of quality is evaluating profit and loss. If we decide to make the required payment necessary to realize our *5-Star Life by Design*, we can expect a profit. If we decide that the price is too high for the life we desire, we can expect a loss. We decide the degree or grade of excellence that radiates from our life. We decide the investment that is required to ignite, inspire, and increase the quality lifestyle we desire.

What Price to Pay

Prior chapters and related activities throughout this book guided our attention to designing a *5-Star Life by Design* that would bring fulfillment and purpose to our existence. We did the homework and the paperwork. Now, we must settle the question, what price are we willing to pay to realize all that we desire and dream? As I was completing my MBA program, the philosophy of my professor was to ask the question "So what?" after each class session. As I bring this book to a close I challenge you with the same question, So What? What cost are we willing to pay to move us to our *5-Star Life by Design*? What profits and losses can we expect?

Quote Your Life's Quality

Quoting Quality is about casting vision. Our *5-Star Life by Design* cannot begin if we don't have an outlook on what we want our lives to be in the future. Do you have a vivid dream of your future or have you stopped dreaming? If we don't dream, we stop living. Living is a progressive journey to an appointed end — not an existence.

If you have stopped dreaming, stopped visualizing, stop anticipating something better and greater — expect loss. Expect a life that is going nowhere, fast. Expect wondering and wilderness wayfaring. Expect life to be drab, dry and deadening.

If you have started to dream again, hope again, and visualize a better future, expect profit. Our dreams, hopes, and expectations are the elements that move us forward. Chapter 2 walked up through the concept and principle of writing a vision statement. Vision moves us toward our purpose.

The Apostle Peter was biased towards the Gentile nation (non-Jews). Peter had a vision of what he considered clean and unclean beast. The vision ended with the God of the universe telling Peter that what God had cleaned Peter should not call it unclean. Minutes later, Gentile servants were knocking at his door for his assistance. Peter's vision enabled him to move past his partiality of people and embrace the prospect of his future.

Unabated Undertaking

An unabated undertaking involves goals and measurements. The term unabated in the American Heritage dictionary means *"sustaining an original intensity or maintaining full force with no decrease."* An unabated undertaking means knowing what you want and going after it. Our commitment compels us to compose in writing the goals and measurements by which we achieve and realize what we see in our mind's eye.

If we don't write down our goals and measurements, our vision remains a dream. We lose.

If we write down our goals and measurements, our vision becomes a starting point to realizing our *5-Star Life by Design.* We have a blueprint by which to build and begin. We profit.

Moses was appointed and purposed to lead the children of Israel out of Egyptian bondage. Moses' one hundred twenty years on the earth included forty years in the Pharaoh's household, forty years being developed on the "backside of the mountain" with Jehovah God, and forty years actually leading the Israelites to their inheritance. At the end of Moses' life, the bible records these awesome words in Deuteronomy chapter thirty four verse seven:

And Moses *was* an hundred and twenty years old when he died: his eye was not dim, nor his natural force abated

The Bible gives this description of Moses, the lawgiver, that his strength and vigor was intact when he expired. A person with purpose and passion doesn't have time to waste away! These people are focused on the end results and accomplish what they set out to achieve.

Inditing Information

Realizing a *5-Star Life by Design* entails having a plan of action.

An architect envisions a construction in his mind. The architect advances the vision by sketching a graphic on paper. The architect fine tunes the sketch until she feels a sense of "ah" in her spirit.

Denying the power of documentation will keep us daydreaming of a *5-Star Life by Design*. We lose.

Deciding to document our *5-Star Life by Design*, like the architect, defines and births the lifestyle we desire. What we write down motivates and moves us to that which we have written. We profit.

Writing this book is a testament to how this concept works. I had a desire to one day write a book. My local church participates in what is called the First Fruit offering. The first fruit offering represents a seed. As I sowed my first fruit offering in 2007, I named my harvest—writing a book. Several weeks later, the Lord gave me the idea of this book. I was ecstatic! My excitement, however, didn't materialize anything. One evening, I made the time investment to research how to write a book. I was overwhelmed with the amount of information that was readily available.

As I read through the material, a resounding theme arose—outlining the book. I set aside an evening to concentrate on the outline. The time investment was less than an hour. I had a plan. I am convinced that God works along with us when we activate a plan of action.

And they went forth, and preached every where, the Lord working with *them*, and confirming the word with signs following. Mark 16.20

As I begin meditating and working on each chapter, the information was drawn to me like a magnet through every day activities: church, work, television, radio, reading, and social events. As I focused on documenting the project, the project materialized into reality.

Accelerated Approach

An accelerated Approach for living a *5-Star Life by Design* involves crafting a process that permits us to move swiftly towards our desires. Accelerating our *5-Star Life by Design* approach mandates that we look at the functionality of our actions in terms of inputs, process, and outputs. When we discover a certain way to do something which results in excellence, we need to standardize those inputs, processes, and outputs so that we are guaranteed excellence every time.

If we fail to accelerate our approach by process management, we waste time, energy, and effort in accomplishing the simplest of tasks. We lose.

If we choose to implement process management, we standardize tasks that yield expected results every time. We profit.

The incredible victory David won over Goliath in First Samuel chapter seventeen serves as a good example of process management. When David volunteered to fight the mighty Goliath, King Saul offered David his military outfit.

And Saul armed David with his armour, and he put a helmet of brass upon his head; also he armed him with a coat of mail. And David girded his sword upon his armour, and he assayed to go; for he had not proved it. And David said unto Saul, I cannot go with these; for I have not proved them. And David put them off him.

David, fortunately, learned the concept of process management. David boldly and wisely stated that he had not tested or worked with King Saul's armament to determine the level of success. David executed what he knew worked. His inputs were a sling shot and five smooth stones. David's process was depending on Jehovah God to work along with him as in the past when David killed the lion and bear (verse thirty seven). David's output is history. David slew the mighty giant, Goliath.

Looking Larger

Riding in an airplane one evening provoked within me a revelation about the way I was living life. I like the window seat. As I gazed out the window, I noticed the activities of those who busily prepared the plane for take-off. I noticed the run-ways that planes were creeping down preparing for departure. As the plane I was on taxied down the runway to prepare for take-off, I noticed the shape of the airport building. When the plane took off, the plane circled back past the airport. I noticed that the view not only gave me a look at the airport but the land surrounding the airport. It was different.

Obtaining our *5-Star Life by Design* requires that we periodically incorporate a larger look — viewing life from fifty thousand feet. Viewing life from an elevated level transports us from silo thinking to systems thinking. Silo thinking functions independently. Systems management functions interdependently. Taking the time to see how every detail of our lives is mutually dependent will alert and alarm us of the activities we consent to.

If we neglect to latch onto a larger look at life, we will be held hostage to the activities that feed into the many areas of our lives. We lose.

If we nurture the notion of systems management, we navigate and negotiate the numerous outputs that could become inputs into the totality of our lives. We profit.

The apostle Paul writes in First Corinthians chapter twelve that the Christian church considers itself as many members but one body. Paul's passion was to position every believer to understand that although we are a "process" within ourselves, we must consider that our output becomes an input into another part or person. We should always remain cognizant of this point because our output becomes an input into someone's process. It is normal to require and demand quality from others. Therefore, we should want to assure that our outputs will be quality inputs for someone else.

I am married to a wonderful person and am blessed to have birthed four children. Everything I do have an effect on my family. My attitude, my goals, and my belief system will produce a positive or negative impact on those living in my home. Proverbs chapter thirty one is a tribute of a woman whose systems management was so well executed that her children and husband unashamedly praised her accomplishments.

Testing Time

I have yet to find anyone who enjoys taking test. An employment test determines if one gets a job or not. A health test determines if one has something to be concerned about. A school test determines if one passes a course or not. A driver test determines if one gets a driving license or not.

Life is filled with tests. We cannot ignore or escape life's evaluation and judgment that determine knowledge, intelligence and skill. Every stage of life presents tests and trials that determine the level of maturity attained.

Living a *5-Star Life by Design* doesn't exempt us from testing times. A quality lifestyle requires that we volunteer to undergo testing to gauge where we are in the process. Turning down testing times risks the opportunity to rise to a greater level of productivity. We lose.

Subjecting ourselves to testing times provides opportunity for operating in excellence. We profit.

The patriarch Job stands as one who underwent tremendous testing. Job was a very prosperous man in his day. Job's testing time involved him losing his livestock, his children, and his health. Job, however, maintained his integrity and stayed the course of living his *5-Star Life by Design*. Staying the course involved further testing of Job by his wife and close friends. Job continued to stay steadfast to what he believed and desired. The end of Job's testing time records this testimony:

After Job had interceded for his friends, God restored his fortune—and then doubled it! All his brothers and sisters and friends came to his house and celebrated. They told him how sorry they were, and consoled him for all the trouble God had brought him. Each of them brought

generous housewarming gifts. God blessed Job's later life even more than his earlier life. He ended up with fourteen thousand sheep, six thousand camels, one thousand teams of oxen, and one thousand donkeys. He also had seven sons and three daughters. He named the first daughter Dove, the second, Cinnamon, and the third, Darkeyes. There was not a woman in that country as beautiful as Job's daughters. Their father treated them as equals with their brothers, providing the same inheritance. Job lived on another hundred and forty years, living to see his children and grandchildren—four generations of them! Then he died—an old man, a full life. Job 42:10-17 (MSG)

Yielding Yourself to Yes

A three letter word stands in the way of taking the journey to living a *5-Star Life by Design* That word is —Yes! Yes implies affirmation and confirmation that a *5-Star Life by Design* is what we want. Yes consents to correcting behaviors that block us from achieving a *5-Star Life by Design*. Yes appropriates acceptable actions that activates ascension into the *5-Star Life by Design* we envision.

Casting off corrective actions conveys staying in the holding pattern that we experience from life. We lose.

Consenting to corrective actions communicates that we have chosen to live a quality lifestyle that sanctions, satisfies, and signifies a higher quality lifestyle. We profit.

The life of the apostle Peter substantiates the positive results of a life that undergoes corrective actions. A fisherman by trade, Jesus selects Peter as a disciple. Peter's character is a marked one. Peter was presumptuous. He was always going beyond what was right or proper. Jesus always provided corrective actions to Peter's behavior. While everyone was sitting comfortable in the boat, Peter asked Jesus to allow him to walk on the water. When Peter began to sink, Jesus corrected Peter that his faith was too little. Self-righteousness prompted Peter to proudly declare that we should forgive others forty nine times in a day. Jesus corrected Peter by telling him he should forgive four hundred seventy times.

When Jesus was demonstrating an act of servanthood by washing his disciples' feet, Peter said "no way." Jesus corrected Peter by telling him if his feet were not wash, he would have no part with Jesus. In an act of militant protection, Peter cut off a soldier's ear when the soldier tried to grab Jesus. Jesus told Peter to put up his weapon. After Peter's training and application of corrective actions, Peter was appointed the spokesperson on the day of Pentecost. Peter's message was so powerful that three thousand persons accepted the message of salvation.

The Ultimate Yes

Living a *5-Star Life by Design* is exciting. A *5-Star Life by Design* is what God has purposed and planned for us. A *5-Star Life by Design* is attainable because the principles of God work for anyone who works them. There is a danger, however, of embracing the principles of God but not embracing the personage of God.

What good would it do to get everything you want and lose you, the real you? Luke 9.25 (MSG)

I invite you to live the ultimate life which is based on the personage of Jesus Christ. His bloody sacrifice is a ransom for those who believe and acknowledge him as Lord and Savior. Accepting Jesus Christ will empower you to live out the principles described in this book. It only takes a three letter word—YES!

Join me in saying this prayer:

Heavenly Father:

All good things come from You. I acknowledge that I have been living my life apart from You. I renounce my deeds of the past. I believe in the sacrificial death of Jesus Christ. I receive Him and make Him Lord and master over my life. I am now entitled to all the benefits of a believer in Jesus Christ. I receive them now, in His Name. Amen.

This simple act of faith has moved you from the kingdom of darkness to the kingdom of Light. I encourage you to join a bible believing church where you can be connected with a support group that will challenge you to grow and enjoy a *5-Star Life by Design* in the earth realm and in the eternal life to come.

It's your time to start realizing your *5-Star Life by Design*. Give yourself permission. Design and Shine!

Notes

Chapter 1

Scherkenbach, William W. The Deming Route to Quality and Productivity: Road Maps and Roadblocks. Rockville, Maryland: Mercury Press, 1991.

Chapter 2

American Heritage College Dictionary, Fourth edition. Boston, Massachusetts: Houghton Mifflin Company, 2004.

Covey, Stephen. 7 Habits of Highly Effective People: Powerful lessons in Personal Change. New York: Free Press, 2004.

Blanchard, Ken and Jessie Stoner: Full Steam Ahead!: Unleash the Power of Vision in Your Company. San Francisco: Berrett-Koehler, 2003.

Warren, Rick: The Purpose Driven Life: What on Earth am I Here For? Grand Rapids, Michigan: Zondervan, 2002.

Sanborn, Mark: <u>The Fred Factor: How Passion in Your Work and Life Can Turn the Ordinary into the Extraordinary.</u> New York: Currency/Doubleday, 2004.

Chapter 4

Tsiakals, Joseph, Charles Cianfrani and John E (Jack) West: <u>ISO9001:2000 Explained, 2nd Edition.</u> Milwaukee, Wisconsin: Quality Press, 2001

Chapter 6

Hilliard, I.V. <u>Mental Toughness for Success: Proven Biblical Principles for Successful Living</u>. Houston, Texas: Light Publications, 2004.

Chapter 7

Blair, Gary Ryan. "Thou Shalt Inspect What Thy Expect." Top Achievement Retrieved October 14, 2007 from <u>www.topachievement.com/gary</u> blair.html.

Chapter 8

Maxwell, John C: Failing <u>Forward: Turning Mistakes into Stepping Stones for Success.</u> Nashville, Tennessee: Thomas Nelson Publishers, 2000.

Printed in the United States
203629BV00001B/199-1176/P

9 781606 473948